LESSON LEARNED...

LESSON LEARNED...

From A Corporate Guy Who Left His Job
To Sell On Amazon Full Time

ROBERT BAGLEY III

ISBN: 1508819106
ISBN 13: 9781508819103
Library of Congress Control Number: 2015903913
CreateSpace Independent Publishing Platform
North Charleston, South Carolina

To find out more about Robert Bagley and RB3, log on to www.
RB3experience.com or visit his YouTube Channel, RB3 Bagley.

PREFACE

H ello, my name is Robert Bagley. Not long ago, I was a frustrated executive who was uninspired in my corporate life and looking to run a home-based business. I wanted the freedom to be with my family when I wanted to be, to work when I wanted to work, and to earn an income that was comparable to my corporate income. So I left my job to sell full time on Amazon and eBay as an ecommerce entrepreneur and I want to share the lessons I learned with you in this book.

Before I made the leap into the world of ecommerce, I was earning a high six-figure salary with a Fortune 500 company. Still, something was missing from my life, and I knew I needed a change that involved not only significant personal risk, but a good amount of faith as well. So, I embarked on what would prove to be the most incredible, life-changing year of my life.

You may be wishing for the same type of opportunity. The purpose of this book is to encourage those who have struggled to find their way. A lot of people go to college and get good-paying corporate jobs, and they think they have made it. Still, they are unfulfilled and lack a sense of purpose. When they hear about the concept of starting a home-based business, they are not sure where to start or where to go.

By sharing my story, I hope to show you how it can be done. I will walk you through how I've gotten to where I am with e-commerce, particularly with eBay and Amazon, as a Fulfillment by Amazon (FBA) seller. This book is not a step-by-step guide or a paint-by-numbers way to get started in e-commerce. Instead, it is intended to be an influencing and encouraging tool that allows you to experience some of the trials and tribulations, as well as the successes, I have had. When you are having a tough day and need some encouragement, I hope this book with provide that for you. Let's begin.

ONE

THE MUSTARD SEED – BEGINNING A

LIFE OF FAITH AND HARD WORK

I was born in 1968 and grew up in the small town of Victor, New York. It's about twenty miles east of Rochester, between Buffalo and Syracuse. It is a Great Lakes city just south of Lake Ontario. I grew up in what they call the Finger Lakes Region.

I feel like I'm sort of a Generation Y person trapped in a Generation X body because I have been blessed to see the Information Age unfold before my eyes, and to be an active and early participant in the new technologies that have mushroomed in the last two decades. I was never the smartest kid in class; I barely got Bs in high school. I hardly ever made high honor roll or anything like that. After I graduated in 1986, I went into college not knowing what I was going to do. It took me a long time to figure that out. I am happy to say that I have found what I love to do and what I believe is the future of business.

When I was five or six years old, we moved from Victor to the much more rural areas of Macedon, and later, Farmington. In Macedon, I went to a one-room school house with grades K-12 all under one roof. In Farmington, my parents built a house about a quarter of a mile back from the road, way off in a corn field. Growing up in the country taught me the benefits and the blessings of hard work. I chopped wood for our wood-burning furnace, and mowed lawns that were really just meadows in disguise. Living in rural areas where folks had to more or less fend for themselves had a lot to do with making me the man I am.

I had a simple but strong upbringing with great parents who loved me and my big brother. He was an All-American cross country runner and two-time Olympic aspirant who taught me to love competition. With his influence and support, I was a four-year varsity runner and track team captain in high school.

When I was sixteen, I started working at McDonald's. I worked weekends and holidays, and by the time I was eighteen, I was promoted to swing-shift manager. I can't overemphasize the value of work experience for teenagers. My job at McDonald's taught me a whole lot more than how to make burgers. I had management and leadership experience starting at a young age. Those are tremendous skills that will last any kid a lifetime.

After high school, I went to Bowling Green State University in Ohio, which was a seven and a half hour drive from my home. Starting in high school and through college, I had found the party life to be my way of living, and it caused a lot of problems. Not to get too deep into this subject, suffice it to say that, like many other young people my age, I did some things I wish I hadn't.

I wasn't sure what to study in college. I started with business administration, but didn't do well with that. In fact, I got a letter from the business school that said, "Mr. Bagley, we think you should reconsider your degree," because I wasn't doing well in statistics, economics, or accounting. That is ironic, because, as an entrepreneur, all of those subjects come into play. Now, however, you can outsource most of those services, and there are so many electronic tools available to help that you don't have to be a whiz in those areas. I am not trying to discourage anybody from getting a business degree; I think it's very helpful. I do use a lot of the things I learned in the short time I was in business school. Luckily for me, I learned more than was demonstrated by my mediocre grades.

I graduated with a four-year degree in interpersonal and public communications. I took classes in theater, persuasion, small-group communication, large-group communication, and one-on-one communication. It turned out to be a great degree for me because I use all of that today.

I worked my way through college and ended up graduating with a 3.0 grade point average. I was on the five-year plan. To earn money, I worked in the hospitality industry. I did two internships while I was at Bowling Green, both at the Hilton Head, South Carolina Hyatt Regency Hotel Oceanfront. I was a food and beverage intern for one semester and the following year was a management intern in the convention services department. All of that gave me great work experience.

A good work ethic is vital for anyone who wants to be an entrepreneur because you have to be self-motivated to get through those times you don't want to work. I am definitely a workaholic; everyone in my life would probably attest to that. I am always looking for more balance there. In fact, this book is based on notes and recordings I made while I was on Christmas holiday with my family. I had already started making YouTube videos telling people about my journey leaving my corporate job and getting into full-time online reselling. A lot of folks wanted to hear more about my story, so I felt compelled, while I had a little downtime, to write a book.

During college, I also worked as a waiter and a bartender. One of the cool things I did was side work for one of my restaurant managers who owned a carpet-cleaning business. When the management companies that owned the off-campus apartments cleaned those units during vacations and in the summertime, we would go in and use machines to suck all of the beer out of those carpets and get them ready for the next semester. That turned out to be a real eye-opener for me. Here was a way to make money that didn't need a big investment or a lot of employees – just a portable extraction machine (think Rug Doctor) and a great deal of sweat equity.

After I graduated from college, I got a job as a TGI Friday's manager trainee in Toledo, Ohio, but I still continued to clean carpets for the same guy. Eventually, I quit the management-trainee job and became an entrepreneur, working as a partner with the gentleman who cleaned carpets. That partnership went sour very quickly for a lot of reasons, but it taught me enough to go back to Rochester in my early twenties and start my own carpet-cleaning business. In Rochester, I moved back in with my parents, which is what so many twenty-somethings do when they graduate from college and still don't know what they want to do with their lives. I went to homes and businesses around Rochester with the one carpet-cleaning machine I had in my pickup truck and did demos for free. I got jobs cleaning residential carpets during the day and commercial carpets at night. I used the connections I had within my family and friends in Rochester, and that picked up pretty fast. I built up the business from just me in a pickup truck with a portable carpet-cleaning machine to having five trucks on the road.

At one point in time, I bought a janitorial company and had fifteen employees. I overworked myself and got to the point where I was very frustrated with that business- too much work for not enough profit. Part of what I did was repair water/flood and smoke damage. I ended up being the subcontractor/general contractor of a franchise called Paul Davis Systems Restoration, which does a lot of work for insurance companies.

Another thing I did, along with my carpet-cleaning business and using the same truck-mounted machines, was to clean awnings. In 1998, I sold my carpet-cleaning business to the Paul Davis Systems franchise owner in Rochester. I got one check for all the trucks except for one – that one I kept.

After that, I became a student of information selling. I met a gentleman named Joe Polish, who got me in front of his mentor, Dan Kennedy, a well-known expert in small-business marketing. I wanted to create my own information products, such as CDs and videos. I took what I learned about the awning-cleaning business and made it a business opportunity in a box. I created how-to manuals, videos, audiocassettes and monthly newsletters. I sold these information products to window cleaners, power washers, and carpet cleaners to help them add the awning-cleaning business to their existing businesses. For about a year and a half, I spoke at various trade-association shows and sold my information-product packages. I sold about $125,000 worth of those packages, which was good, but the flip side of those sales was not too pretty. It cost me about $225,000 to make that $125,000 in sales. And I was in deep - I had pumped all the money I made from my carpet-cleaning business into the information-product business.

The Internet was just starting in 1998, and I had some products online, but at the time, I didn't do much with them. I was selling cleaning agents and sealers via a shopping-cart website. Back in 1998, I thought I was really cool to be using this kind of edgy technology. Problem was, I don't think I got one order from it, and I was running out of cash . One day, I got a call from a representative at DuPont Flooring Systems. He asked if I would be interested in becoming their employee and setting up a carpet-cleaning division. I desperately needed cash, so I did that. I had gotten myself pretty deep in debt using personal credit cards and such and had to claim bankruptcy. So I had some peaks and valleys going on there.

I took the job as the general manager of carpet maintenance for DuPont Flooring Systems. They were setting up commercial carpet stores in different markets, and one particular flooring store wanted to add carpet cleaning as one of its offerings. I did that for about a year and a half. I started from scratch, selling the jobs commercially as well as doing the jobs myself because we didn't have enough jobs to hire employees. I was making $40,000 a year. At least it was income. I needed the stability because I was getting married. Having the job helped me recover a little bit from my financial distresses.

I quickly grew that business from zero to $30,000 a month in sales, and I was able to hire an operations manager and a couple of technicians. During that time, something amazing and life-changing took place in my life.

TWO

FINDING LOVE, FAITH AND MORE MONEY

My wife Larisa, who is a hairstylist, had a client who kept asking her to go to church. She kept telling the client, "I don't know. My new husband probably won't want to go." She was right. At that point in our lives, we weren't seeking out any kind of religion or spirituality.

On July 11, 1999, Larisa was invited to an outdoor church service in Rochester, New York, by Lake Ontario. She told me, "Let's just go, it's outside and maybe she won't ask us anymore if we just go." It was a gorgeous summer day. An evangelist named Nick Costello, who was a part of the emerging Billy Graham evangelist society, got up and gave his testimony. He had been a rock star, playing the bass guitar for a national recording band called Toronto back in the eighties. He lived a life of sex, drugs, and rock 'n' roll, which was similar to our party lifestyle that I described earlier.

After the church service, we were bound and determined to go and waste the rest of the day getting drunk at my father-in-law's birthday party. At a family gathering like that, we would normally have about a six pack and some shots apiece, along with pot and even some other "things." But, as Nick Costello got up and shared his testimony about how God changed his life after he received Jesus Christ as his Lord and Savior, a lot of that resonated with me. I was brought up Roman Catholic, and what Nick was saying about Jesus Christ as the basic foundation of faith hit home. Then, Nick did an altar call, asking people in the audience if anyone would like to come up and say a prayer to receive Jesus as Lord and Savior. I had never experienced anything like it. Larisa and I looked at each other as if to say, "I will go up if you do." We both rushed to the altar and gave our lives to Jesus. That was more than fifteen years ago, and I can happily tell you that our faith has been a strong part of our lives and marriage ever since.

We left the church service not really knowing exactly what had happened to us. We arrived at my father-in-law's house and walked up to the door. Once inside, he handed me a beer. It was like the devil was on one shoulder and an angel was on the other saying, "Are you going to take that?" we had used drugs and alcohol for about sixteen years of our lives, and I am happy to say that we have been sober for more than fifteen years. That is a really good thing if you are prone to excess like I am. I tend to be compulsive in a lot of ways. I can't do something a little bit; I have to do things in excess. So having a clear mind really helps make good decisions, and being sober has been a big part of that. I thank God for his strength and guidance.

I knew something supernatural had taken place because Jesus took away the desire I had for drugs and alcohol. I am certainly not judgmental of anyone who claims religion and still drinks or smokes in moderation, which I believe a lot of people can do. I cannot.

Larisa and I grew quickly in this church. We didn't have kids yet, so we started taking new believers' classes at the church. Within a year, we started a small group, and I was leading it. I started picking up the guitar and playing worship songs, too. Twenty to twenty-five people would come to our little house. We would even go out in the middle of the winter to pick people up and bring them in, feed them pizza, feed them God's word, and then take them home.

I was still working at DuPont. I was watching some of the carpet manufacturer's reps come in to the DuPont offices and show the commercial carpet they were selling. I wanted to do that. They had company cars, were able to work from their home offices, and made good money selling carpet. I wanted to get out of the cleaning business, start selling carpet, and have a lifestyle like that. So I began putting my résumé out. At the end of 1999, I got a job with flooring manufacturer, Mohawk Industries, as a commercial carpet rep and worked from my home office. I really enjoyed that because it combined my entrepreneurial drive with the stability of a big company backing me.

I was working hard at my job, and also learning and growing in my faith and in the church. I believe that for anybody who has faith in his or her life, work is not separate; it is all one. And I believe that everything we do has a reason and a purpose; our faith and our work are intertwined. In the scriptures, the disciples were actually fishermen, and they were in the market-place. That gave them a great platform from which to share the gospel. My faith informs everything I do, from my church involvement to my performance at work. I let my clients and colleagues see my faith in how I lead my life. If someone asks me to share my story, I would do so willingly.

As a new manufacturer's rep working for Mohawk Industries, I learned how to do outside sales. I was pretty darn good at it. Going to see flooring dealers was like running a milk route, but it was really nice that I was able to do that by day and learn my faith at night. Larisa and I were still taking classes at the church and hosting small groups at our house. One of the men in our group was a good friend and spiritual leader named Robert Blackhall. He was from England and had gotten transplanted to Rochester several years before I met him.

I learned how to sell flooring and carpet cushion in outside sales. I had a pretty big territory that covered much of of central New York, and I would call on about sixty different flooring dealers. I would get them to buy display programs, sample programs, stocking goods, rolls of carpet, and rolls of cushion. It was a good working ground for me to understand outside sales. And when you own your own business, you are always in outside sales. It was my first crack at doing a corporate sales job that I liked.

Nine months into my job at Mohawk, a representative from Shaw Industries, a competitor of Mohawk's, approached me. Shaw, the world's largest carpet manufacturer, had six different commercial brands at the time and was a multibillion-dollar company. Mohawk is the world's largest flooring manufacturer when you add in all the different surfaces of flooring they sell. Shaw was starting to branch out from selling just carpet to offering hard surfaces, like laminate, hardwood, and ceramic. They were looking for outside sales reps to be dedicated to their hard surfaces. This was right at the beginning of the century, and I took on the new position at Shaw in September 2001. If you were alive at that time, you know that it became a very turbulent time in our history as a country. It certainly made me a little nervous going into a new job when the World Trade Center towers came down on 9/11. Eventually, the economy picked up a bit, and the job was a pioneering opportunity for me.

The territory was doing $300,000 in sales, and I built it up to about $1.5 million in sales by calling on flooring dealers and getting them to buy display programs, sample programs, and stocking goods. The products included pallets of laminate, hardwood, and ceramic, as well as underlayments, adhesives, and other supporting products.

At Shaw, I received accolades as a hard-surface rep and was named Salesman of the Year for a couple of years in a row. I received other rewards as well. From 2001 to 2003, I was making $50,000 to $60,000 plus expenses.

I was getting good training as a building block in my life. Additionally, I was forming relationships with customers, convincing people that laminate flooring was hot, as well as other products. Laminate is still on the market today, but it was hard back then because it was a relatively new product category. I had to convince people to take pallets of laminate goods and try them. Eventually I got a few people connected with our laminate program and quickly started to sell truckloads of it, but I really wanted to get back into selling commercial carpet.

When I was still with Mohawk, Larisa and I went to Israel for a twelve-day prayer and missions trip (March/April 2000). We absolutely loved our experience there. Prior to us going, Larisa (who was told all of her adult life that she could not have children because of endometriosis) was healed in a Church service and it was confirmed by exploratory surgery. The doctor came out and said, "Your wife has been healed, you can start to try in a few weeks to have your first child." Miracle of miracles, we conceived in Jerusalem, Israel, and nine months later, we had FaithAnn, our miracle child. As you will see a little later, FaithAnn became an integral part of my decision to get into the e-commerce business.

THREE

NEW BEGINNINGS—

NEW YORK TO CALIFORNIA

In 2003, my pastor and mentor Robert Blackhall, whom I mentioned earlier, mapped out a plan for me to get more involved in ministry. This was when I was at Shaw Industries as a hard-surface rep, before the company let me transition back into commercial carpet sales. One of the steps on our checklist was for me to go to seminary. Lo and behold, I got accepted to a seminary in Rochester. It was a newer one—only five years old at the time. It was attached to Robert Wesleyan College, a private liberal arts Christian school.

In 2003, I started working full-time at Shaw and going to school full-time. In 2005, I earned a Master's Degree of Arts in Theological Studies. I am grateful to Shaw Industries for helping me earn my degree by reimbursing me for a large part of my tuition. With the support of my management leadership, the company decided to help me because the program offered good opportunities for me to increase my leadership skills. I went through eighteen months of extensive church history, from the resurrection to the twenty-first century. I had to read mounds of theological papers and studies and write a ten-page paper every week. In addition to leadership, I learned about listening and building relationships, and discipline. God was preparing me for many things in the Church and the marketplace.

It was a great time. I don't know how I got through it, but I was in my early thirties, so I was still young and had substantial reserves of energy. During this time, Larisa and I were blessed with our second daughter, Mandi, who is 19 months younger than FaithAnn.

I asked Shaw to let me transition into commercial carpet sales, and they agreed, making me a sales rep for their Designweave brand. I started with $200,000 in sales and built it up to $1.4 million. In my first full year, I increased sales $1 million. Certainly, outside sales is a great career, but you are going to find, through my history and my story, that online sales is something I am even more passionate about.

When I graduated from seminary, I left with wonderful knowledge, a joyful relationship with God and a passion for leadership. I began submitting my resumé to Shaw to be considered for a sales manager position. I had loved outside sales, but I knew I was ready to try new challenges and to guide, direct, coach, train, and develop salespeople. It took me about a year and a half of circulating my resumé within Shaw and other companies eventually to land a Regional Vice President of Sales position at Shaw, still with the Designweave brand which later became Patcraft.

Here's how it happened. In September 2007, one of the Senior Vice Presidents (Steve Decarlo) who knew I wanted to get into leadership called me and said, "Hey, Robert, I think I know the answer to this question, but would you like to be a regional vice president?"

I said, "Absolutely."

"OK, here's the rub. Basically, you will have to go home to your wife and give her five choices: New York City; Orlando, Florida; Seattle, Washington; Denver, Colorado; or San Francisco, California."

All of those locations were open because the company was going to promote five new RVPs within this brand.

It was a great day, getting that call. That night, I went home and presented those different locations to Larisa. We put it before the Lord, and it was tough. We are both from Rochester, New York, and were brought up here. Our families are there, too, so a move to any one of these big, and in most cases, distant cities was a radical idea. Larisa said she would consider all of the locations except for San Francisco, which seemed so far away and culturally foreign to her. "But go ahead and put your name in the hat for all five, and let's see what God will do," she told me.

Three months later, after multiple interviews and a lot of waiting, we got the call from David Vita (the hiring manager and soon to be my new boss), and guess which location he said we got? San Francisco! We began to transition the family and sell the house. We had an executive relocation out to San Francisco, which eased the process a bit, particularly for my wife and children. It was 2008 when we started to build a house out there and move. That was a really rough time for real estate, and we moved into the county that had the highest foreclosure rate of any county in California. I started work as soon as I got the job, but it took about six months to get my family there, so I commuted back and forth from San Francisco to Rochester every two weeks.

It was hard for all of us, but I was learning a ton in my new job, so we bore it and considered ourselves lucky for the opportunity.

One of my first duties as RVP was to reorganize competing reps within the different Shaw brands into one team instead of having them work as lone wolves. Now, they were going to hunt in packs. It was a big change and I had to put several people on performance-improvement plans. I also had to let a number of people go.

One year, seventeen sales reps were reporting to me, and we generated about $33 million in sales in a couple of showrooms that I oversaw in the city of San Francisco. It was a great time for transforming me into a leader. I was learning how to manage, coach, and develop salespeople. I didn't enjoy the job's heavy paperwork and administrative load, but quite honestly, it was a great experience. It is hard going from sales to sales management. Most companies promote their best salespeople to sales managers, but good sales reps don't always make good managers. I was sure trying, and achieving a level of success I felt good about.

As she expected, Larisa and the children never felt truly at home in California, but we were there four and a half years, and we were happy, because we were together. However, during that time, Larisa's mom got sick and passed away suddenly. We all wanted to get back to the East Coast knowing it might be inevitable in the carpet and flooring industry because all the companies are headquartered there. I began to put my feelers out to try to get a job within Shaw on the East Coast. Mohawk, the Shaw competitor I had worked for early on in my career, happened to have a position in sales training. I thought, *Boy, that would be a good thing for me because I have a passion for training.* I love to help people, and as a regional vice president, I was developing people in their sales skills. I focused on that during my interviews and got the job. Senior Vice President of Mohawk Commercial, Jay Imperatori and his boss Michel Vermette hired me on.

Mohawk moved us from San Francisco to Atlanta in 2012. Another new season began for us.

FOUR

DREAMS AND DESTINY

I have had several dreams in my life, especially since we started walking in our Christian faith, that I call "God dreams." These are dreams that are very vivid, have a lot of meaning, and are worthy of journaling. They do not necessarily happen when I am asleep. If you are not journaling in your spiritual life, you should. Journaling is a huge part of reflecting on everything. So whether you are a believer in a religion or faith or not, you should journal your thoughts. It's like keeping any other form of diary. I have volumes of journals. Lately, I have been slacking on that a little bit, but creating this book is a form of journaling for me.

I had the first dream about a decade ago. I was at a Christian conference and was staying at another attendee's beautiful house. At midnight, I was walking around in their backyard and doing what I call the "pray-walk." I was looking up at the stars and worshipping God. In this waking dream, I looked up and saw the moon. I was saying, "Oh, God, You are so good, You are so big, You are so awesome." All of a sudden, that moon started to spin around. It turned into the world, then came down and hovered over my hand. The world was spinning in my hand. I have been so moved by that image. After I told a friend about the dream, he replied, "Robert, God has given you the nations." In fact, this statement is coming true in our Amazon business, as we will be selling in Canada and possibly Japan soon.

I had another dream right as we were moving to San Francisco with Shaw. It had to do with the Christian faith and a lot of other different faiths. The number eight played an important part; eight suggests new beginnings in Hebrew.

We closed on our brand-new house in San Francisco on August 8, 2008. If you write that out numerically, that's 8808. Even more significant is that the night before - August 7, 2008 - I had another "God dream." At that time, the economy was going crazy with all of the bad mortgages written. It was a tremendously uncertain time in this country, and Larisa and I were feeling our share of that uncertainty, not knowing the area we were moving to or any of the people there. The night before we closed, the stars were shining brightly. I was looking up, worshipping God, and thanking Him for His goodness. I was walking ankle-deep in the ocean, barefoot, praising God for His goodness and vastness. All of a sudden, I imagined that I was taken up into the sky, flying like Superman. Someone had my arms and my hands, and some-one else had my feet, and I was flying parallel to the ground. I would say I was at an elevation of about fifteen thousand feet. I was soaring through the air, and I was thinking, *This is so cool! What is this? Why am I so blessed to be taken up like this and to have a ride like this?* All of a sudden, I started to freefall, and then my thoughts went to, *Oh, God, what is this all about? I am freefalling straight to the ground.* Right before I landed on the ground, it was almost like someone scooped me up and gently placed me back into the ankle-deep water, and I started walking about. I thought, *God is so good. Wow, thanks for the ride!* I looked up, and there was a huge angel in the form of bears in the sky. They responded to me, saying, "You are welcome." That affected me deeply and motivated me to search the scriptures to understand what it was all about.

Here is what I found. Several weeks after my dream, I was walking on the treadmill while reading my Bible. I went to Psalm 91. Basically, it says, "He will assign his angels over you, and they shall bear you up in their hands lest you dash your foot against a stone." The word "bear" stood out to me because of the bears I saw in my dream. The next day, as I was telling somebody about my dream in a restaurant called The Black Bear, he said, "Well, the state animal of California is a bear."

In putting all of these details together, I felt that God was saying, "Hey, in the midst of all the tribulations and trials, in the times that you feel like you are freefalling, I've got you in my hands, and I've got you covered. I'm going to set you back down gently into those peaceful waters in the midst of your freefalling in your mind."

These experiences have stuck with me as I go through the roller coasters of life. They remind me that no matter how far I feel like I'm falling, God has me, and He will scoop me up and set me down gently before I crash and burn. My faith in his abiding strength and presence has comforted me and lifted me up in my new life as an e-commerce entrepreneur.

FIVE

New Beginnings Again—

From California to Atlanta

O nce I received the brand-new job as Director of the Sales Academy for the Commercial Carpet Division of Mohawk, I commuted from California to Atlanta for about six months, just as I commuted from New York to San Francisco when I got the job with Shaw. Eventually my family moved to Atlanta and we lived in temporary corporate housing for 3 months while we found a great home in a fantastic tennis/pool community in Northeast Georgia.

At Mohawk, I was given a white canvas to develop training materials for new sales reps. In a short period of time, I set up an online university and an onboarding program for carpet sales reps in the commercial division. I blended multiple phases of live training with online and classroom instruction, as well as field training. In about three years, I was able to move one hundred carpet sales reps to the commercial division. In phase-one training, we'd walk our new reps through how to sell, position Mohawk, explain the brand, and share product knowledge. I teamed each new rep with a more experienced salesperson who would partner with them back at Mohawk and help them on a daily basis. We all gathered in Dalton, Georgia, so that the teams could meet one another. It was very rich training, and we received a lot of great feedback from it. We even made *Training* magazine's list of the top 125 training companies. When I was there, we made it into the top five every year. This really helped us develop curriculum around sales training for these particular reps, and it was enriching to be able to make a positive impact on about 250 young men and women getting started in their careers.

To add to the regular training curriculum, I would interview subject matter experts on different topics and then create podcasts of those interviews. The reps all had company cars in which they could listen to MP3 files. When I traveled in the field, I noticed that a lot of them were doing that. I also set up an audiobook program composed of 5,100 recordings so that they could do self-guided training. It was a holistic kind of training, with topics ranging from business to parenting.

I have always benefitted from listening to audiobooks for both learning and pleasure. If you like to listen to books, I suggest you get *The Wal-Mart Effect: How the World's Most Powerful Company Really Works—And How It's Transforming the American Economy* by Charles Fishman. Another one I like is *The Everything Store: Jeff Bezos and the Age of Amazon* by Brad Stone. If you are in retail sales, read and listen to books about retail because it is very important for your development.

At Mohawk, I equipped all the sales reps to be self-training. To help do this, I created some videos I called the "two-minute advantage," which were composed of two to three minutes of tips from subject matter experts. My sales reps loved those. I took my own advice: every week or so, I watched a video and learned something about a new product or a training tool we were using.

I love to use video and audio to help people because they can look at it or listen to it at their leisure. I try to keep it short and sweet. You can put a little bit more content into audiobooks because people have more opportunities and time to listen to them, such as when they are exercising or driving, than they do to watch videos. I call it "taking windshield time and down-time and turning it into personal and professional development time." There are always pockets of time when you can feed yourself knowledge to encourage and develop yourself in specific subject areas. Currently, I have been putting on webinars about how to do things such as how to use webinars and other training and development methods to reach out to various audiences.

My position as director of sales training at Mohawk was really an office job with a lot of administrative work. I missed being in the field and doing field coaching and development. I got the chance to speak and train live, but that was only about 5 percent of my job and that was the part I loved! Also, during that time I was certified to teach Franklin Covey's *The Five Choices of Extraordinary Productivity* and *Four Disciplines of Execution.* It was fantastic material. I was a student of high-level execution and of time and energy management. Using weekly report sessions conducted online, I helped people identify important goals and track lead and lag measures on those goals. It was a powerful program I suggest you check out.

Earlier I mentioned FaithAnn, our miracle daughter who was conceived in Jerusalem. At one point, it became difficult for FaithAnn to participate in gym class and otherwise be active because she developed pain in her joints, hands, arms, and legs.

She twisted her ankles repeatedly and had pronated (flat) arches. We went to several specialists. In Atlanta, a doctor said she needed surgery on one foot and surgery on the other foot six months later to strengthen the ligaments and to place artificial arches in her feet. We felt that it was the right thing to do.

Unfortunately, the surgery proved to be a significant shock to her system. She developed a condition known as RSD (Reflex Sympathetic Dystrophy) which totally shut her down. The condition caused her to have extreme pain up and down her body, especially in her joints. Whether it was physiological or physical didn't matter to her; the pain was real. She stopped playing the piano, writing, and even taking showers on her own, all at the young age of eleven. She became a special-needs child who required nearly constant attention from Larisa. I was busy with work. The medical bills began building up, and even though I was making a strong six-figure salary, we were also working to get out of debt, recouping from the loss we had to take on the sale of our house in California.

Larisa and I went through Dave Ramsey's financial management program, and, as a result, we were able to knock out about $50,000 in credit-card, vehicle, and student-loan debt. We were trying to avoid going into debt again, so I tried to get a part-time job on the weekends. The places I wanted to work required work hours during the week, and I couldn't do that. So I searched online for a business I could do from the house at my convenience. As a result of my research, I set up two websites: Bob's Best Books and Bob's Golf Store. They were affiliate websites, which means I got a commission for every customer I brought in who ultimately made a purchase that was fulfilled by either Amazon or Ebay. I was drawing people to Amazon and eBay listings, trying to make commissions from affiliate sales. I won't get deep into that, but it required a lot of time and energy and did not generate much return.

One day, at my community's garage sale, a woman and her daughter were looking through my old seminary books I had put up for sale. The woman seemed to be scanning the books with her cellphone. This seemed so strange to me that I asked her about what she was doing. She said her husband was going into the seminary and that she had started a part-time business with her daughter to offset some expenses. I was curious about what she described as her part-time business, so I researched it and found Rob Anderson's *Dollar Moves*, which talks about setting up eBay and Amazon businesses. He had some YouTube videos in which he teaches people how to send books from home to Amazon and resell them. I took that challenge and sent in $89 worth of books in November 2013. The sale of those books is what got me started selling online. And it all started because of mounting medical bills.

Sometimes, things that you feel are a curse turn out to be your biggest blessings.

Six

The Year of Change Begins

After I discovered that I could sell things online, I knew that setting up my business would be the best way to work part-time to supplement my full-time corporate job. I needed to keep us out of debt and to have the flexibility to work when I wanted to. That is one of the advantages of online selling and e-commerce. I kept the two websites I was running—Bob's Best Books and Bob's Golf Store—so I could continue to dabble with the affiliate marketing platform, but I was determined to become an FBA, or Fulfilled by Amazon seller

With Fulfillment by Amazon and eBay, you have to buy and list products and also pack, prep, and ship products. It is labor-intensive, but the rewards are great. I am going to walk you through some of the sales numbers. My first month to try this was November 2013. That month, I sold eight books on Amazon and received $89. In December, I sold $215 in books, and in January 2014, sales shot up to $851. They took a dip in February, and

March went down to $718. I had a lot going on at work, so I had to scale back.

Then something amazing happened. In April 2014, I went from $700 in book sales up to $3,300. At that point, I had started retail arbitrage, which is the process of finding products at brick-and-mortar retail stores to sell online at a profit. Recently, I've gotten into online arbitrage, which is buying products online and reselling them online for a profit, but so far I have not had great success with it. I am reading Chris Green's book *Online Arbitrage*, which you should get. He also wrote a book called *Arbitrage*. John Groleau, who has become a mentor of mine, has published a few books on the subject, too.

In April, I stumbled upon Retail Arbitrage (buying products in retail stores, then selling them on Amazon) as I was watching some videos online. I joined a Facebook group called Scanner Monkey. Jay Bayne started the Scanner Monkey reseller membership group and also does a *Spreecast*, which is an online interactive video forum. I was watching all sorts of FBA Spreecasts, from Barrington McIntosh to Chris Green to Peter Moelius, and, of course, Scanner Monkey.

That is when I stumbled on the Amazon Seller app, which is free if you sell more than forty items per month. You pay Amazon per product to sell on the website. I still use the Amazon Seller app to scan products.

Here's how retail arbitrage works. One day in March, 2014, shortly after I started selling online, I went to a Staples office supply store and started scanning items with the Amazon Seller app on my cell phone. I then purchased the items at their sale prices and resold them on Amazon at regular price. In little more than a day, my sales shot up to $333! That was my first effort to dabble in retail arbitrage. I continued doing it, and in April, my sales were $3,300. In May they shot up to $8,800, and in June, my sales totaled $11,577. Remember, I did this part-time. People were asking me, "What is your profit?" At that point, I was making 20 to 30 percent profit. I was skimming off a little bit to pay some bills and putting everything else back into the business. Everyone needs different profit margins to operate their businesses. If you can make 20 to 30 percent net profit, you are in good shape. A lot of business owners on the stock market are happy if they run a 12 to 15 percent margin. You could probably do more as you get more experience in this business.

In short time, I was receiving orders for about 543 items per month. I offered products ranging from paper towels to Nicorette gum. Six months earlier, I had started off by selling just eight products a month. In July, sales went up to $14,745 with 712 products sold. Business was really starting to pick up momentum. I started going deeper into retail arbitrage and began selling toys and games—again, I was just scanning everything. I would go to Walmart, Costco, Toys "R" Us, Staples, Rite-Aid, Walgreens, and several other stores. Target was a big one; I scanned a lot of items there. If you are just getting started, scan everything. My motto is simple, and I got it from Tim Baucom of Shaw Industries: he always told me, "Sell as much as you can for as much as you can." I used my profits to buy more products, sell more, and then turn around and buy more. That is what you are going to have to do, especially if you are working from a tight budget like I was.

At one point, I infused about $4,000 into the business with a loan from my 401(k) plan, then used that money to jump-start the business. My sales jumped from $21,000 in August to $22,657 in September. I paid the loan off quickly. At that point, I was working on the business about thirty hours a week and working thirty to forty hours a week in my corporate job. That was a problem. I could not dedicate the time and energy I needed to my corporate job, and I realized that my passion no longer existed for it. I was tired of commuting an hour to go push a pen behind a desk. So, one fall afternoon I walked into the senior vice president's office and said, "I think it's time for me to move on. My heart is not in this anymore. It's not good for the company, and it's not good for me."

He asked if I had another job. I told him I had a side business reselling books and doing some online arbitrage stuff. I said I wasn't sure exactly what I would do next; I just knew I needed to move away from my existing job and make a transition. You know that when your heart is not in something, it's not worth it to continue. Life is too short to be doing something you don't want to do. And I knew that with my business generating almost $23,000 a month in sales part-time, that this thing had life. If I was going to sell or work for anybody, I really liked the prospect of selling and working for myself, like I used to in my twenties, when I had my cleaning business.

That Senior Vice President had been instrumental in helping me get into Mohawk and helping us with the transition in California. His name, as I mentioned earlier, is Michel Vermette, and he had been a mentor and friend. Based on the strength of our relationship, and the value I had brought to Mohawk during my time with them, I asked him for a severance package to give me some time to figure out what my next move would be. He said he would get back to me. Two weeks later, he came back to me and said, "We trust that you don't have another job with a competitor, that you do sincerely want to leave and figure out what you are going to do next, and that you need time." They gave me several months' pay, which really helped out. Folks, don't shy away from being bold. I always say, "You have not because you ask not."

September is a really good time to leave a corporate job to do online reselling full-time. Make sure you have a good year of understanding the business part-time first and then, if you are going to jump off the cliff like I did, you really want to do it at a time when the volume is going to start picking up, and that is exactly what happens in September.

After generating $23,000 of sales in September, my first day of working in the business full-time was at the end of September. My goal was to spend $1,000 a day in October on sellable inventory so as to invest in future earnings, rather than taking immediate profits. In gearing up for the big Christmas selling season, the last thing I wanted to do was sell out my stockpiled inventory and not be able to restock before the big selling season ended.

I really wanted to see a $30,000 month in October. I am happy to report that I did $29,377 in October, my first full month of being full-time. You can see some of my videos on my YouTube channel, RB3 Bagley, where I track this out. You might be wondering how I could make so much by spending $1,000 a day and making $1,000 a day. Remember, this was the first time I was ramping up for a fourth quarter, not knowing what I needed to do. I gained knowledge by watching what some of the other professional resellers were doing. There were Facebook pages that advised spending $1,000 a day from September to January to continue to ramp up for the volume that was going to be coming for Black Friday, Cyber Monday, Cyber Week, and Green Monday. I will talk about those later.

Remember, this was just FBA sales. I exceeded $30,000 in sales because I had several hundred dollars' worth of eBay sales.

Again, I was just selling books and CDs on Amazon, and I was selling on eBay just to learn eBay. To this day, I am infatuated with eBay and still have listings there. I have gone antiquing with some professionals to learn the value of things. I met eBay guru Danni Ackerman when she came to Atlanta. She travels the country to show people how to find items that will result in bigger profits. Her website is at www.thedanniapp.com. I have learned a lot from her and others like her.

My goal was to hit $40,000 in November. I am happy to say that I came close by selling $39,800 worth of product—$38,740 in Amazon sales and a couple hundred dollars in eBay sales. What a difference a year makes! I did $89 in sales in November 2013 and had $40,000 in gross sales in November 2014. It's just a huge testimony. By the end of December, 2014, I showed $78,674 in gross sales. Can you believe that? It is just incredible! My total for the year was $231,476, most of which was done part-time. I worked full-time in this business for only two and a half months of that time. I hope this encourages you.

The scriptures talk about how God blesses us above and beyond anything we can ask or think. This business is definitely one of those cases, and my daughter's recovery is another. As I mentioned, our older daughter, FaithAnn, struggled with RSD after the surgery she had. A year ago, as of this writing, she was not able to take bathe herself.

We watched her struggle through this, but around the time my e-commerce sales grew and I started to work from home more, FaithAnn began to get better. She was writing and playing the piano again. She also started playing the clarinet and guitar and taking voice lessons. She bought herself a guitar and has learned to play it and now sings beautifully. She really loves the arts. She has been the videographer for some of my videos.

She loves videography and using Video Star, Eye Movie, and YouTube. After she celebrated her thirteenth birthday, we saw great leaps of improvement.

I have been at home more and have been more available to go on longer vacations with my family. I can shut off the business when I want to and turn it back on when I want to. In fact, I am writing this chapter in my father-in-law's basement rec room in New York, where we are visiting. While it is nice to be able to see family and friends, it is also beneficial that I have been able to keep up my FBA online sales work the entire time I have been here. One of the most attractive aspects of this lifestyle is that you can work from anywhere – the technology makes it possible. What a difference a year has made, not only in the business, but in the life of my family and the restoration of health for our daughter.

I want to encourage you that you can grow this business at your own pace and take it anywhere. It can really transform your life and your family's lives.

SEVEN

WHAT I HAVE LEARNED SO FAR

Now that you have heard my story and have seen that I was able to quit my six-figure job to do FBA and a little bit of eBay selling full-time, I will share what I found to be good and what I would not do again, plus some numbers to illustrate the growth and timing of the process.

By January 2015, when I pulled some of the final figures, I showed a $10,000 loss for the year. Losing money in a new business the first year is not a bad thing because I paid myself and paid off a lot of bills. I chalk up that loss as a learning curve. Hey, if you go to college, even if you spend only one semester learning something, it still has value. Hopefully next year will be in the black and not the red.

The Saturday before Christmas, I had more than two hundred orders averaging $44.87 per order. With FBA and eBay combined, sales were more than $9,000 for the day. About 75 percent of those sales were in toys and games. The remaining sales were of household products and groceries. For December, we exceeded $80,000 in sales —$79,870.83 on Amazon and $500 on eBay. Our goal was $45,000, so we certainly went above and beyond anything I could have asked or thought would happen. I did have to sell some items at a loss because I wanted to move them and the prices had tanked. I'll share some of that in a little bit. Before overhead costs, the gross profit on the cost of goods sold was $16,000.

In 2014, total annual sales were $232,393. Remember, for almost ten months of the year, I did this work part time. That's not bad, doing almost a quarter of a million dollars in gross sales while working in the business full-time for only three months. Almost all of those sales—99 percent—were on Amazon (FBA). Of that total, 35 percent of sales was health and personal products, 17 percent was office supplies, 16 percent was toys, 6 percent was groceries, and 5 percent was clothing.

As you can see, that 5 percent in clothing represented multiple products that I didn't have much competition on because most people won't go through the process of getting "ungated" in gated categories on Amazon.

What does it mean to become ungated in a category on Amazon? In order for Amazon to keep professional resellers on their website, Amazon makes its resellers demonstrate their understanding of the more complicated listing and sales requirements of certain product categories. Getting ungated in the different categories—shoes, handbags, sunglasses, watches, clothing, automotive parts, DVDs, and video games—really paid off for me this past year.

The gated category approval process is complicated and can be time-consuming. I went through twelve denials before I finally got approved. I finally hired a consultant to help me get ungated.

Now she does all of my ungating work for me, and it is well worth the money I pay her. Many people are making their livings helping resellers get approved in gated categories on FBA. If you want help with any of your gated categories, I suggest you go online and search for services that do category approvals for FBA.

Now, I will share some things I've learned. I am going to get specific about some products here and what I did early on. Again, selling products on Amazon in the fourth quarter of the year is critical because almost 50 percent of online sellers' annual gross sales happen in October, November, and December. It is just how it is if you are an online retailer.

I had no idea what I was doing, so I joined an online Facebook group led by Jessica Larrew called "Q4 Prep Group" (see Jessica's info in the Resources section as I bought many programs from her that helped tremendously!). I didn't participate as much as I wanted, but I did glean a few tips that really paid off. For example, I learned the importance of having padded envelopes ready to do merchant fulfillment during the holidays. I also learned that I bought retail toys and games off the "hot toy list" way too early. I spent up to $5,000 doing that, if not more. If you have cash invested in something, you have to let it go at a loss at some point so that you can recoup some of that cash and pump it back into inventory. As hard as it is to sell at a loss, you need to do that for the sustainability of your business long term.

Here's a case in point. I did well on Target and Walmart's exclusive Disney *Frozen* products, that were not available to Amazon, as well as some of the nonexclusive items that were listed on Amazon, up until Cyber Monday. I bought one nonexclusive item – a singing Elsa doll - for $28.99 and sold it right before Thanksgiving for $63. I sold about thirty of them. Then, on Black Friday, so many resellers went out and pulled them off the shelves, the online market was flooded with them. After Cyber Monday, the price tanked down to $35. It stayed there a while, then got worse, and Amazon finally sold out of them. I finally just dumped it. I lost $10 per doll, and I still had twenty-eight in stock. Ouch!

You need to have the right products stocked prior to Cyber Monday, and then you can gauge the marketplace – what is selling at what price - from there. It seems as if Walmart and Target reflooded the shelves on Black Friday, so the resellers gorged themselves on the products, and then it became a race to the bottom. You need to have the profitable products stocked up, and you need to watch trends. Go to the Amazon price-tracking websites www.camelcamelcamel.com or www.keepa.com to look at pricing histories. And read. The toy and other consumer product industries have trade publications that are very informative and offer an insider's perspective.

The big winners for me were clothing and accessories. I sold socks, shirts, sunglasses, some handbags, and some shoes, but most of it was clothing. I sold pullovers, hoodies, and T-shirts. Again, I didn't have a lot of competition on those items, so I was able to sell a lot of them and make really good profits. I would buy several pairs of socks at a wholesale club for $9.99 and sell them for about $23, or even as high as $30, tripling my profit. I did very well on the Target exclusives, but not so well on the Walmart exclusives. Target had some sets of six *Paw Patrols* action figures, and I did really well with those. I did really well with some Target-exclusive Barbies but not so well on others. I did well on nonexclusive Disney *Frozen* dolls and some Elsa and Anna dolls, but those items tanked after Cyber Monday. A few of them did retain their value because they were hard to find.

I did really well with video games and Legos, although I got burned on a few Lego products. I bought too early because I didn't do my research. When Target sold Legos for 20 percent off, I bought some. They had a promotion whereby if you spent $70 one week, you got 20 percent off of your sales the following week. I bought ten of the Lego sets when they were available, and the following week, I used my 20 percent discount on anything I bought in ten different Target stores. I would go to five stores in one day and ask them to do two different transactions. I bought tons of Legos. I would scan them with the Amazon seller app, and if they were making a little profit, I grabbed them. I could use my 5 percent Target discount debit card and my tax-exempt wholesaler's status, which gains me another 6 percent discount. I always take my sales tax certificate with me, to make sure I can get my tax-exempt discount. With all these combined discounts, I could save 20 to 30 percent and sometimes more.

Here's another technique I used. Sometimes Target would run specials whereby if you bought two popular video games, you got a $50 gift card. I used my 20 percent coupon in the electronics section. You have to buy video games at the electronics checkout stations. I bought approximately $1,000 worth of items at each store and got tons of the $50 gift cards. With those cards, I bought Legos with the 20 percent discount. So that became extremely profitable for me.

My mom had a vintage Hess Oil tanker truck collection. She was going to give them to Goodwill. When I told her how collectible they were, she contributed them to my business. I listed the items on Amazon, and they sold like hotcakes at $35 to $45 dollars apiece. Gross sales were about $1200. Best of all, everything was pure profit!

I do a lot of my sourcing at drugstores, like Walgreens, Rite Aid and CVS. One week, Walgreens had a promotion called "Jingle Cash." If you spent $100, you got a $20 coupon to spend. So that week, I hit all the Walgreens stores. This was three weeks before Christmas. I wasn't buying things at a loss; I was making sure they were already profitable on Amazon. Then I would load them into my cart and buy them.

EIGHT

TOUGH LESSONS

A s you can see, the first year as an online seller was a wild
ride for me. As a businessman, the old excitement I had
missed was back, as well as "all-in" engagement and focus. It was
thrilling and I loved it. I felt that, at last, all was right with my
world. But I was wrong. In fact, I was so immersed in my new business I did not even realize how wrong I was. It seems that, somewhere in my decision process, my enthusiasm for this new way
of doing business, with its independence and opportunity for
profit, caused me to lose sight of the two most important things
in my life; the things that are, in fact, my reasons for living: my
family and my faith.

Earlier in this story I described the "all-or-nothing" aspects of
my personality. From my youth as a track and field athlete to today, my philosophy has always been, "Go big or go home." In my
career, that belief in myself and my abilities has led me to consid-
erable success. In my personal life, however, before I found the
wisdom and strength gained through my faith community and

relationship with God, that philosophy sometimes meant me getting drunker than anyone else.

I jumped into the world of online selling with an enthusiasm that took even me by surprise. In my mind, something that felt so right to me must surely be just as appealing to Larisa. I barreled along, making plans, and later choices, that were about one thing only: my vision for my life, and how I chose to provide for my family.

In spite of her initial doubts, Larisa supported the new business, and was happy for me in my newfound excitement for being my own boss. However, as I have described, I left my corporate job, with its 401K plan and health insurance benefits, at a time when one of our children was struggling with a debilitating physical condition. I made a mistake in that I did not include her in my decision process the way I, as her husband and friend, should have. That hurt her deeply.

It goes without saying that any decision made that does not take the happiness and well-being of both spouses into equal account, is one made without the prayerful seeking of the gift of discernment. I have said before in these pages that I cannot separate my work life from my life of faith, and I failed to adequately seek God's guidance before I made this decision. I have apologized to Larisa, my children, and to God for acting unilaterally. I thank Him daily for the grace and blessing of my wonderful wife.

I have included this last section as an object lesson. While I want you to know that it is possible to achieve success as an online entrepreneur, the transition into the "flying without a net" life of running your own business is not one to be taken lightly. There will be significant changes, in big things like financial security, as well as little things, like being at home and underfoot all day. More than anything else, it is vital that your loved ones are on board before you take the leap.

Here are my recommendations for anyone who is considering making the leap to full-time reselling. I call them,

Robert's Rules for Reselling

1. Make sure you have complete buy-in from your spouse before leaving your job!
2. Have at least six months living expenses and three months of business expenses banked.
3. Credit Cards are Dangerous! I know that people justify using credit cards to buy products to resell because of the rewards points. However, the temptation to put off payments is too great, especially if it comes between having to make a decision to pay yourself out of necessity or paying the credit card in full that month. The credit card payment will lose that game every time!
4. Once you feel you're ready to leave your job and the above criteria are met...stay in your job 3-6 months longer.

Robert's Pros and Cons of Selling on FBA Full Time:

Pros:
1. Work when you want to work.
2. You can now dedicate full time attention to sourcing and inventory management.
3. Ability to scale the business by having time to train others to take over repeatable tasks freeing you to concentrate on sourcing product.
4. Capability to control your destiny by having time to diversify into wholesale buying, private labelling your own

products, subscribing to and buying from online lists, etc.

5. Have more time to network with other resellers by going to local meet-ups, conferences, and joint shopping excursions.

Cons:

1. Cash Flow. Always buying inventory to grow business. Two week payouts from Amazon can be tough to manage cash.

2. Having to pay yourself for a full time household income (if you have to do that like I had to). The minute you leave your job, you have to start taking money out of the business to pay yourself and you can't use that money for operating expenses and inventory anymore. This can stunt the growth of the business significantly depending on your salary requirements.

3. Hard to get another stream of income because FBA can be all-consuming.

4. Inventory replenishment and maintenance – as you increase your SKU's & listings, you have to watch stock of these products so you don't run out and make sure they are always priced appropriately. The marketplace on Amazon fluctuates 24/7 and so does the pricing of your inventory. These activities become a larger part of your time and attention and it's difficult to outsource these activities.

5. Retail arbitrage (going to the physical stores to buy goods) becomes a job – it can be long hours away from home – unless you can outsource the shopping which is

hard to do the first year or two while you are learning the business.

<u>Last Thoughts</u>: At the time of publishing this book with current events unfolding constantly (June 2015) I am about to accept a job to go back into Corporate America. Whether I continue with FBA part-time or not, I'm not sure. I am looking at Kindle Publishing as a viable part-time e-commerce solution as it is truly a laptop lifestyle business. FBA can be if you do strictly Online Arbitrage, Wholesale, and or Private Label and send all your goods to a fulfilment house that preps and ships your goods to Amazon for you. However, the capital outlay in any FBA business is extensive as opposed to Kindle Publishing where you can hire ghost writers to do projects for you at between $.01-$.05 per word – much less capital needed with huge potential for returns and truly passive income. I'll keep you posted through social media on all of this.

My hope is that, after reading this book, you will have more insight and information to make a solid decision on Fulfillment By Amazon either part time or full time.

Best Wishes To You!

The Following Section Are The Transcriptions of Several of My You Tube Videos During the End of 2014

Video 1
Building Your e-Commerce Business with "replens" - Replenishable goods

Hey, everybody, it is Robert Bagley with a Tuesday Tip on how to build your FBA and eBay e-commerce businesses frequently replenished goods, or "replens". As some of you may know, I just dumped a $200,000-plus job to do this full time, and I am trying to do it enough to get up to that same income level. And the way I am doing it is with replens.

So I want to talk to you about how to build your business with replens today. I will be checking my notes so that I don't miss anything. The first thing is, challenge yourself to go out there and get some replens, whether they are grocery items or dry goods, something that can sell and you can count on selling week after week after week. Go out and find a few, scan a few. Listen, they may not be the big-hit profit margins you are looking for. You may have to compromise a little on your profit margin, but you are still going to make somewhere between $2 and $4 profit on each. These are not high-cost items, but just go out and find something. I double-dog dare you to get about ten to fifteen replens in the next two weeks and watch your business start to grow. What happens when you build these replens is that it builds stability in your business, and you can count on some of this annuity business coming in. After mixing in some higher-margin stuff, you can go after BOLOS and things that are not going to see a constant turnover.

The other thing is, when you get a replens, test it, see if it works. If it's working, go get some more, and then keep testing it.

Watch your reports; you can always go in and pull a weekly report and look at your parent request on your parent items, and it will give you a report. Pick the dates and the ranges to see how many you are selling each week, and then you can gauge how much inventory you need. Don't get more than you need. Try to anticipate sales so you are not getting too deep into it, but man, don't run out of them. Watch how many are selling, anticipate that, and go out and get them and keep them in stock. That is the key to replens—don't let them run out. Watch those levels and parent item listings in your reports, and be just crazy about keeping replens in stock. I double-dog dare you!

The other thing is, always be on the lookout for new replens. Why? It grows your business and builds a steady foundation for repeat business. What happens is, 20 percent of your Replens fall by the wayside. You always need to fill the pipeline with some new ones. Why do they fall to the wayside? Hey, maybe a competitor got on that listing, and it is no longer profitable for you. Don't get married to it, but study it and learn it. Maybe there is a like item that you can get in on. That's the beauty of Replens: it helps you diversify your business and keeps you investigating. The cool thing is that every Replens and every product you sell is like its own business. And that is pretty cool because you can learn the trends on that particular product, and again, you can learn like products. Go out there and get ten to twenty new replens in the next couple of weeks. Maybe they are just grocery items or dry-goods items. Maybe multipack them; maybe there is already a multipack listing. Go out there and find some, and always be on the lookout for new ones because, again, they are going to turn over.

I hope that helps. Good luck in Q4. We will talk to you all very soon. Robert Bagley signing out. Bye.

Video 2
My First Day as a Full-Time FBA Seller

Good morning. It's Robert Bagley, and today is the very first day that I am not reporting to my corporate job. It is September 29, 2014, at 7:00 a.m. My wife's nephew, Richy, is behind the camera. Hi, Richy. Say "Hi." After our first video last night, this is our cheesy whiteboard. People commented and said, "Hey, Robert, you are at $22,000. That's great, but most people don't start off at $22,000."

So I want to take you down a little bit of our numbers since we started. I started with books back in November 2013 and did $98—all part-time while I worked my full-time job. We tripled that in December 2013, to almost $300. In January, it jumped to $900, and in February 2014, we dipped down to $745 because my corporate job got busy. In February and March, we were in the $700 range. From March 2014 to April 2014, we went from $784 to $3,570. That is when we started retail arbitrage. We tripled that the very next month—from $3,500 in April to $9,400 in May. This is all this year, folks. We did start from scratch; I just want everyone to realize that. From $9,400 in May, we went up to $12,000 in June. Nice jump there. From June to July, we went from $12,000 to $15,000 and from $15,000 in July to $21,800 in August. Again, I did all of this part time myself, with a little help from my eleven-year-old doing labor.

In September, we are almost at $21,000 with two days left to go. So it looks like we are going to break $21,000. We are about to do a shipment this morning. We are gearing up for Q4, so right now we are trying to spend about $1,000 a day to ramp up to where we need to be with our income, which means we need to be processing about $1,000 a day to keep up with the shipment. That is our goal: to ship every day. Last night we were busy.

We have some monster Franklin boxes ready to go out. UPS is going to come get them. We have signed up for Smart Pickup from UPS. We are just doing a couple of pickups from here and there for now. And we have about twenty boxes going out this morning. We still haven't moved into the basement yet; we are still operating from upstairs. I just want to let you know that this can be done. And now that I am excited to put my full-time efforts into this, until the next video, go get them, ground hustle, and don't get discouraged. This is a great business. Bye.

Video 3
Gross Sales in December 2014

Happy 2015, everybody. It is Robert Bagley, RB3, here, wishing you a happy New Year. It is January 8. I want to give you a recap of how things went with the Christmas selling season, the end of 2014, the end of Q4, and really, the end of my first year of doing FBA. I'm going to try to keep this under fifteen minutes and talk pretty fast. Hopefully you can keep up with me.

First we are going to go to the results. I am going to share some notes with you that I wrote here. The Saturday before Christmas was our biggest selling day of the year; we had over $9,000 in sales that day. About 75 percent of it was toys, and the rest grocery, health, and personal care. We had two hundred orders at $44.87 average net selling price.

December numbers—I don't know if you remember from my previous video before this, my goal for November was $40,000, and we hit $39,000, which put our December goal at $45,000. We did $80,000 in gross sales—pretty cool. I still have some overhead to take away from that, but of that $80,000, about $15,000 to $16,000 was gross profit. Not bad. We are showing about a $10,000 loss for the whole year. I chalk that up as learning, and not bad for $232,393 in gross sales for 2014. Remember, nine months of that, I did it part time while I worked at my corporate job; I was full time for only the past three months.

Some of you may know that the reason I started this business was because we had gotten ourselves in personal debt. We were starting to pile up some medical bills, and I can tell you later how to find out more about my story. Long story short, I wanted to try something part time, and the jobs I wanted to do, people wanted me to work shifts during the week. That just wasn't going to work. So I started on my journey to find out how I could sell online on my time, and that was pretty cool. I found out in the end that not only was it a great part-time income, but it became my full-time job. A lot of you are tracking that along with me. I think we are at week seventeen or eighteen; I've lost track. It's January 8, 2015. I left my corporate job and began my first full day of full-time work with FBA (Fulfillment by Amazon) on September 23rd.

So in 2014, again, just shy of a quarter of a million dollars in gross sales—$232,000. Of that amount, 35 percent was health and personal products, 17 percent was office supplies, 16 percent was toys, 6 percent was grocery, and 5 percent was clothing. And there were some other uncategorized things on top of that. But those were the big sellers.

I am going to talk to you about some of the things I learned early on. I went out and bought retail products that we got paying retail using hot toy lists. Not a good idea. I ended up dumping a whole bunch of Zoomers that came back damaged from Amazon, and I was issuing some refunds and such after the Christmas season. Not too bad, but everyone warned me. I won't be doing that again. I just went out with hot toy lists and bought the For Real Pets, the Zoomers, and some of the Disney *Frozen* things. I also bought some Legos. Some did well, and some didn't. Some of you saw that I bought the American Girl dolls. I bought them off the website for $115 each and sold them for like $190; that worked. Some of the Legos didn't work because I bought them foolishly. Some of them really worked well because I bought them right—I used coupons and such during the Christmas season.

One of the things I noticed was that after Cyber Monday, stuff started to tank. In other words, all of the products that did well for me did well only up 'til Cyber Monday. Then Walmart and Target reflooded the shelves, and it seemed like resellers just gorged themselves on these, and then it was a race to the bottom. Prior to Cyber Monday, I bought them for $28 or $29 each and sold them for $60. The highest was at $63, right around Thanksgiving. After they tanked at $28, and in the stores that way today, even though I did really well up until that, I actually had to dump twenty-eight of them yesterday. If you know anything about FBA, you know I am losing $10 a doll on that. So, hey, I am not going to do that again. I am going to find out what's working prior to Cyber Monday, and I'm going to be very careful about what I stock between Cyber Monday and Christmas.

I think if I were going to do this all over again, I would really build up for Cyber Monday. That means I am not going to buy the Zoomers and the Legos I scanned prior to Cyber Monday that are showing a profit on Amazon. I did buy them in hopes that the price would go up and Amazon would run out, but that never happened on some things. Some things I did really well on are the Target and Walmart exclusives, specifically Barbies, Cop Patrol, and some of the Disney *Frozen* stuff. Again, you've got to be gated on some things like Disney *Frozen*. It is well worth doing if you can invest in toys and games that are exclusive at Target and Walmart. That helps you to know that Amazon is not going to get on those, but certainly anybody and their brother can go out and buy those and sell them as a reseller. So just go out and test it—test, test, test, scan, scan, test, test, test.

The big winners for me, again, were Target and Walmart exclusives; those are really good. Clothing is great for me. It costs a lot of money to get ungated because if you want to do it yourself, you have to be a genius, I'm not good at that. You have to do flash files and all of this other stuff. I had to pay a consultant to get me ungated, and that was the best money I have spent. If you are scanning products that you are not approved for or you are restricted from selling, go online and find out who can help you become gated. There are all sorts of services—Google, Amazon Approval—that will help you get approved in different restricted categories. So just take on a couple of those keywords.

Talk about a business that grew out of thin air. If it were me, I would get ungated on everything because you just don't know when you are going to come across a product you don't want to be restricted on, especially during Q4. I am so grateful that I got unrestricted and approved in DVDs and video games. I rocked with those during Q4; that was really cool. Clothing: I sold socks, I sold shoes, I sold underwear (women's and men's), men's shirts, pullovers, pull hoodies—those did really well for me. So, you say, "Where do you source for those?" Anywhere. I like the wholesale clubs for clothing. You can go to Walmart or Target to source clothes; you can go to Ross, TJ Maxx, and Marshalls. You've certainly got to scan a lot for it, but go there.

Another thing was Hess trucks. My mom had a collection of Hess trucks that she had been collecting for decades. She gave me about twenty-five of them to sell as a contribution to our business, and they did really well. I think we listed them on the seventeenth of December, and we had four or five of them left. All of them sold for between $35 and $65. Awesome—pure profit there. Take donations from family; it helps. Again, video games, some Legos, some of the drugstore retail arbitrage I did really paid off. Just watch, and you can figure that out yourself. Everybody has different drugstores around: CVS, Walgreens, Rite-Aid, etc.

My goal for 2015 is simply to go deeper into retail arbitrage. How do I get to a base of $45,000 a month of Replens? You can watch my video on "Replens Is Back." But that is what I want to do—I want to go deep. To do that, it is going to take a lot of leg work. I am also going to get into private labeling. There are a lot of private-label groups. I am going to do some more with wholesale buying, and I definitely want to go deeper in some of the categories I am approved in and ungated in. I have not gone in deep with jewelry, clothing, or shoes. I want to go deeper in those. But really, folks, my biggest goal is retail arbitrage. You can do online arbitrage, you can do private labeling, and you can do wholesale—those are great. But I think you need to earn the right to do those by really building up your retail arbitrage business. I am going to do that. I recommend that you do it, too.

[I've added this section since as the goal needed updating. The other big thing is, I am going to create a book of what happened this past year (this is the very book I'm discussing in the video – GOAL ACCOMPLISHED!) I think it is just going to be a story from my upbringing until now. A lot of people don't know me and my past, and I would like people to know that. Hopefully it will be an encouragement, so look out for that. Please support me in there.]

Also, I am going to go to the gym more, and I am going to invest in my marriage. My wife and I are going on a cruise this year. I will invest in my family and be dedicated to taking the time to be with family.

I want to wish you all the best in 2015, and I just want to leave by thanking a few people who really helped promote me and get this YouTube channel up: Paul Ash Begal, Chad Pagel, Alan Chumpski. I want to thank the people from Scanner Monkey: Jay Bayne and Cornelia Blake. And Andy Slamans, thank you for your Spreecast. Peter Molius. I love your Spreecast that got me started. Monica Wiseman, a new friend of mine, has a private-label group and helped me with my thoughts on private-label products. Rich Fluegel, my employee who put up with all of the stuff I brought back, listed it, packed it, and got it ready for shipping. John Groleau—I am a part of his group, and he has helped rocket my business. Thanks, John. Awesome job. You are the man! Sam Cohen who is a HUGE inspiration to all resellers as he will do over $10 million in gross sales in 2015 and has a new coaching group. Sam has always been there for me from when I was still working a corporate job up until now. You're the best Sam! Jessica Larrew—I was in her prep group. Thank you, Jessica. Karen Locker has helped me with a lot of my ungating and ongoing processes on FBA. Thanks to Danni Ackerman for helping me, encouraging me, showing me how to make money on eBay. And, of course, my wife and kids for putting up with my obsessiveness.

Again, best wishes to you and thank you for reading this book. If you are reading this and you want to dabble in FBA part time, I highly encourage it. You never know; it might become a full-time gig for you and it could offer you the freedom and the ability to be very successful. Good luck in 2015, God bless, and until next time...RB3 signing off.

Video 4

HOW RB3 Sold $16,869.91 worth of product in a Week

Hi. It's RB3. Happy holidays, everybody! I am dressed in holiday gear here, and believe it or not, it is December eleventh, and it's 32 degrees—brrr, cold degrees here. I wanted to give you guys an update and go to the RB3 whiteboard to check out the Q4 tracker. I have a bunch of things to share with you about numbers and what I have learned this week as we continue to progress.

I believe we are at week number twelve since I left my corporate job. If you have been tracking it in any of my videos, you have seen that we have had some goals and some progress. I left my job right before Q4, which is probably a pretty good time to leave your job if you are going to do this full time and start Amazon and eBay. I also recommend that you pay off as many of your bills as you can, have no debts, and have three to four months' cushion if you are going to do this. That way, you can have some money in the bank so that you can really put some money into the business and keep it moving forward. But certainly if you are going to jump off a cliff to do this full time and leave your job, you can do it. I show that through my videos.

I had a full-time job that paid over six figures, so we are trying to prove that this can be done.

In November, we had a goal of $40,000. We just missed it. No, we are not real sad about that because we were pretty darn close. If you recall from the previous videos, in October we did $30,000 and so to increase it in November by $10,000 in gross sales, that is great. Again, highlights were Black Friday, $2,100 for the day—not exactly what I expected, but I have never done this. This is my first fourth quarter, so I didn't know what to expect. Then we figured, "Hey, if we did $40,000 in November or close to it, then we should certainly be able to do $45,000 in December." We are definitely on our way to doing that.

So, let's take a look here. Cyber Monday in December is kicking off the month. Huge day. We talked about this in my last video. Almost $5,000 for the day, so pretty good, but I know some people with Spreecasts and Scanner Monkey who did $20,000 for one day. So maybe we will hit that next year; that would be pretty cool. But there is this phenomenon called Cyber Week; it really kept moving until about Friday. That is what I learned. And Friday was Cyber Week, so Monday, Tuesday, Wednesday, Thursday, and then Friday, Saturday tanked. It was like the faucet shut off. But in the midst of it, we did almost $17,000 for a week. I never thought we would be able to do something like that because previous to that, I think our best week was $11,000. So, pretty cool, Cyber Week. Out of that, we had about $300 in eBay in Cyber Week. So eBay sales were picking up because we are still learning eBay. We are really an FBA company, but we are definitely moving some product on eBay.

The Monday after today is what Amazon is calling "Green Monday." We are already feeling the increase in sales today, December 11, 2014. So, wow! All of these names: Black Friday, Cyber Monday, Cyber Week, and now Green Monday. What does that mean? That means it is going to pick up from December tenth to the eighteenth. We are already seeing this happen, and in talking to a lot of experts and veterans who have done many Q4's, this is what we can expect. We can expect this surge again. So, Cyber Week and then it dies down, and then this whole new phenomenon of Green Monday and everything that leads up to it.

Let's talk about a few things I learned this week. I put a restricted product up and got a policy violation from Amazon, but it wasn't our fault. We didn't realize it was restricted because their system allowed us to send it in. Be careful. You want to be very sure of what you are sending through Amazon. Even though sometimes it says you can list it, just make sure. Double-check as you are putting your listing up because you don't want to receive that policy violation and then have to work to get it reversed. We were actually approved to sell it. That is another thing I want to say: save all your e-mails that Amazon sends you because then you can use those e-mails as proof. Sometimes the computer at Amazon just does things, so you have to put real proof in front of real people to prove that the cyber robots wrong, if you will.

The other thing is sales and coupons, oh my! A lot of this stuff we did on eBay included some restricted DVDs that were approved. You do have to get ungated for them on Amazon. But there are certain items they will still gate. This particular one, believe it or not, was the Disney DVD *Frozen*. We couldn't sell it, but Target was giving out coupons. If you sold $75 worth, you got a free DVD. We got seventeen free DVDs and sold them all on eBay for $14.99 to $16.99 each. We played around with the price, but the majority of them sold for $16.99. Definitely during the holidays there are all these sales and coupons. One week, if you bought something worth over $70 at Target, you got a $20 coupon for the following week. We got ten of those, so Rich, who is shooting the video—say, "Hi," Rich—he and I are going to go spend those. Walgreens has a promotion called "Jingle Cash." If you spend $100, you get $20 toward the next week's purchases, and they did that two weeks in a row. I think we got twenty of those. So you can really start getting product. We also bought Park Barbies at Target for $14.99 each and got eight free ones. By the way, those Barbies are selling really well at $35, which was a really good flip. These are free, and I am selling them for $11.99. We have seven or eight of them and already sold a couple of them.

I am going to end the video here with a couple of online arbitrage clips. This whole phenomenon of Green Monday I just learned about because I went on Amazon's website. Amazon is the Wall Street where you buy and sell on some trading stock exchange, if you will. Peter Moelius made that comment on Andy Slamans's Spreecast, which you should check out. Those two guys and Harvey Speck talk about their $20,000 Cyber Monday.

I bought a watch for $49.99 at a Green Monday sale. It has a rank of nine on Amazon, and we are going to be flipping it for $79.99. You can buy only one. I bought two Olympus cameras on Amazon for $179.99 each. Again, it was a Green Monday sale, and when it was gone, it was gone. They moved fast because you can't get them at that price now. We just listed them this morning for $265. Of course, you have some Amazon fees and such in there. But I like arbitrage. Certainly you can buy and flip stuff on Amazon.

I may not see you all until after Christmas, so Merry Christmas, and we will see you next time. Good luck, and good selling.

ABOUT THE AUTHOR

Robert Bagley—or "RB3," as he was known in the corporate world— and his wife Larisa have been married for fifteen years and have two daughters. FaithAnn is thirteen years old, and Mandi is eleven. Robert owned several businesses in his twenties and then went into corporate sales for fifteen years. He was an executive salesperson, a regional vice president of sales, and most recently a director of sales training with Fortune 500 companies in the flooring industry.

Robert started a part-time e-commerce business to pay some medicals that were plaguing his household, even though he made a strong six-figure salary. That business now employs family members and does a robust five figures in gross sales monthly.

A seminary graduate, Robert is also a trained preacher and pastor, roles he serves voluntarily for churches across the country.

He is documenting his departure from corporate America on the YouTube channel "RB3 Bagley," and he now has a weekly show, "The RB3 Show," on the same channel. You can learn more at http://bit.ly/RB3Bagley. Also, visit www.rb3experience.com for all of Robert's ongoing projects. Additionally, a video of one of his sermons is available at http://www.godtube.com/rb3bagley/.

ACKNOWLEDGMENTS

First and foremost, I want to thank God for giving me an incredible life that is now being made known to lots of people. God has shown me how to move into my destiny and teach others to accelerate into theirs!

Next, I want to thank my wife, Larisa, on whom I constantly drop things out of the blue, like, "Honey, I left my corporate job today to sell online full time!" Yikes. I thank her also for putting up with my obsessive work habits and late nights of work. I want to thank my daughters, FaithAnn and Mandi, who put up with my being distracted many days yet still love me.

I couldn't close this book without thanking the people in the reselling community that I am grateful for and who have helped me along in my journey. First and foremost is John Groleau, who wrote *Adventures in Arbitrage*. You can Google it or look for it on Amazon. He has been a great inspiration. Jay Bayne, the founder of Scanner Monkey; Cordelia Blake; and Ken Blake, a good friend of mine who put together an Amazon tour in Chattanooga, continued to speak encouragement and wisdom into my life. Andy Slamans has a Spreecast called "Slamazon," and he has a private-label course I am working on now. I appreciate Chris Green for prompting me to document everything. He is responsible for inspiring me to create the YouTube channel and this audiobook. Peter Moelius and Ryan Wateska got me motivated early on with their Spreecasts. Danni Ackerman has a website and hosts "A Day with Danni." She has been an encouragement and has taught me how to make money on eBay. I thank Jessica Larrew for the information she shares freely; it has helped me make money. She charges, too, but hey, you have to make a living.

A big thanks goes to Karen Locker, who is not just a virtual assistant but a business partner. She is the one who helps me with the Amazon ungating approval process. She works on my storefront on a monthly basis as well. She is always there to bounce good ideas off of and steer me in the right direction on many things when I veer off. Rich Fluegel, my part-time employee this past year, has worked tirelessly on listing, packing, and prepping all of the stuff I go out and buy, and he has done a great job.

I would have never endeavored to put this book together in all its formats without the encouragement of Chris Green, author of the wildly successful book *Online Arbitrage*. I also want to thank Sam Cohen for his advice and expertise as no one I know sells as much as he does on Amazon! Additionally, I want to thank Cesar Gomez, James Benner, and Bea Bee Bab administrators of the RB3 Game Changers Facebook Group and co-producers of my show "The RB3 Show!" for supporting me in the midst of a lot of adversity and pushback from many directions.

Many other people have helped and encouraged me along the way, so if you have done that, thank you!

RECOMMENDED RESOURCES:

This link will take you to my webpage where I list all products and resources I recommend to help you in learning and growing an ecommerce business:

http://bit.ly/RB3RecommendedResources